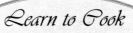

Poultry

Learn to Cook

Poultry

Barbara Beckett

HARLAXTON

Page 2: Tandoori Chicken is grilled or barbecued and presented at the table on a bed of spicy rice and garnished with coriander (cilantro). The preparation is shown on the endpapers.

Published by
Harlaxton Publishing Limited
2 Avenue Road, Grantham, Lincolnshire, NG31 6TA
United Kingdom
A Member of the Weldon International Group of Companies

First Published in 1994

Publisher: Robin Burgess
Project Coordinator: Barbara Beckett
Designer: Rachel Rush
Editor: Alison Leach
Illustrator: Kate Finnie
Photographer: Rodney Weidland
Produced by Barbara Beckett Publishing
Colour Separation: G.A. Graphics, Stamford, UK
Printer: Imago, Singapore

British Library Cataloguing-in-Publication data.
A catalogue record for this book is available from the British Library

Title: Learn to Cook, POULTRY
ISBN: 1 85837 081 7

Contents

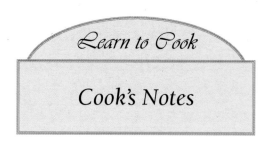

Cook's Notes

Measurements

As the metric/imperial/US equivalents given are not exact, follow only one system of measurement within the recipe. Standard spoon and cup measures are used in all the recipes, and all spoon and cup measurements are level. I recommend using a graduated nest of measuring cups: 1 cup, ½ cup, ⅓ cup and ¼ cup. The graduated nest of spoons comprises 1 tablespoon, 1 teaspoon, ½ teaspoon and ¼ teaspoon. For liquids, use a standard litre or imperial pint measuring jug, which also shows cup measurements. Ovens should be preheated to the specified temperature. The heat on top of the cooker (stove) should be set at medium unless otherwise stated.

Ingredients

A 1.5 kg/3 lb/size 15 chicken is used for all recipes. Fresh fruit and vegetables should be used in the recipes unless otherwise stated. **Herb** quantities are for fresh herbs; if fresh are unobtainable use half the quantity of dried herbs. Use freshly ground black **pepper** whenever pepper is listed; use **salt** and pepper to individual taste. Use plain (all-purpose) flour unless otherwise stated. Fresh **ginger** should be used throughout, unless ground ginger is called for. Use fresh chillies; if substituting dried chillies, halve the quantity. Cold-pressed virgin olive **oil** is recommended, but any type may be used. Use unsalted butter. Preferably use fermented wine **vinegar**; however, cider vinegar and malt vinegar may be substituted if preferred. White granulated **sugar** is used unless stated otherwise.

Stir-fried Chicken with Walnuts is a quick and easy dish to make. Most of the time goes in the preparation.

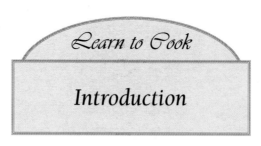

Introduction

A piping hot roast chicken, surrounded by crisp roast vegetables and a savoury sauce laid out on the dinner table ready to serve to family and friends—what a delight it is! And what great pleasure we can give when sharing a homemade meal. This book will teach you how to cook poultry even if you have never cooked before. It explains the basic steps as well as cooking techniques you may not have tried before or feel a little nervous about trying.

The instructions are clearly set out. There are step-by-step guides to the different cooking methods, such as poaching, braising and grilling (broiling). Many of the recipes are photographed in preparation stages to show a special technique as well as what the finished dish looks like and how to present it for the table. Detailed step-by-step drawings also illustrate how to truss a chicken, joint a duck or carve a chicken. There are handy hints, giving information such as how to make clarified butter and how to use it, making a bouquet garni, thawing poultry and deglazing the sauté pan.

The recipes are cross-referenced within the book. For example, there are several different sauces to serve with poultry, so you could continue to roast a chicken in the usual way but experiment with the sauces to get a different flavour each time. Likewise, there are different types of stuffing. Enjoy experimenting once you have mastered some of the techniques.

A glossary of cooking terms is on page 47 for you to look up any term that is unfamiliar. There is a list of recipes on page 5 for your reference. Be sure to read the information on measurements and ingredients on page 6.

The recipes are drawn from cuisines all over the world: India, China, Italy, France, Thailand and the United Kingdom. There are recipes for roasting chickens (broilers), poussins (spatchcocks), turkeys, ducks, guineafowls and quails. Geese are cooked the same way as large ducks.

One of the most important things to do when trying a new recipe is to read the recipe very thoroughly before starting. Check that you have all the ingredients, and make an estimate of the amount of time needed. Have you time to roast the chicken? Or would it be simpler to joint it and sauté it with a pan-juice sauce? All the chicken recipes are made with a 1.5 kg/3 lb/size 15 chicken. If you have smaller or larger birds, adjust the time slightly and keep testing for 'doneness' (see p. 10).

Chicken is one of the most readily available meats and relatively cheap. It harmonizes with a variety of flavours, offering endless culinary treats. If you can, buy free-range chickens—they taste so good and are so succulent that you don't need to add many condiments for a fine flavour. A simple Roast Chicken, French Style (p. 12) flavoured with tarragon and served with mashed potatoes and parsnips is a meal fit for the gods. When using battery or frozen chickens I tend to put more flavourings into the dish as well as moisture.

It is economical to buy a whole fresh chicken and joint it yourself; you can cook some straight away and marinate the rest or freeze it. I prefer to have a variety of chicken meats,

Chicken Schnitzels (p. 31) are chicken fillets flattened out with a rolling pin and dipped in beaten egg and breadcrumbs. Pan-fry quickly in hot butter and oil and garnish with capers, Parmesan cheese and lemon wedges.

rather than all drumsticks or breasts; but you can please yourself, as all are available these days.

Never keep an unfrozen chicken for more than two days before cooking, and store it in the coldest part of the refrigerator. When storing, take it out of the plastic bag and wipe it all over before putting it on a clean plate with a sheet of greaseproof (waxed) paper over. Never keep it in the plastic, as it sweats and bacteria may develop.

No special equipment is needed for cooking poultry, though it is handy to have poultry shears to cut up birds. Very sharp knives, and a range of them, are a necessity in any kitchen. Metal skewers, large and small, are handy. Saucepans and frying pans (skillets) are far more efficient if they have thick, heavy metal bases and tightfitting lids. The thick base ensures even cooking and retention of heat. It is worth while investing in a food processor if you are serious about cooking, because it saves so much time and energy.

Well now, enjoy yourself and good cooking!

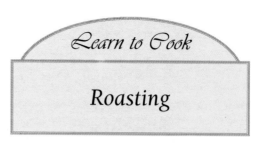

Roasting

A roast chicken or duck is one of the great joys of cooking and always gives an air of festivity and shared pleasure, even though roasting is one of the easiest cooking techniques to learn. Always preheat the oven before roasting. It is generally better to roast at a high temperature in order to sear the meat and crisp the skin. Trim the birds of any extraneous fat, inside and outside. Wash and pat dry and season according to the recipe. Add salt to taste at the end of cooking, never before, because it can dry out the meat.

Nowadays trussing is not recommended, as it could prevent the bird from cooking evenly through and thus run the risk of bacterial infection. If you need to truss—to make the bird look its best by keeping the legs and wings close to the body—tie it up loosely with string (p. 42) and make sure it is thoroughly cooked, with no pink meat.

Cook the bird on a rack placed in a roasting pan, preferably over butter, oil, wine or chicken stock (p. 44). To get a really crisp skin, baste every 10–15 minutes with the pan juices, and make sure the pan juices don't dry up—they will be needed for the gravy.

Test the bird for doneness by pricking the skin of the thigh in the thickest part with a skewer; when the juice runs clear and not pink, the bird is done. A small chicken will take about 1 hour, a large one 1 1/4 hours. See individual recipes for cooking times for other poultry.

After the bird is cooked, it should be rested for 15 minutes in a warm place to allow the juices to be absorbed back into the flesh. Make the gravy in the meantime.

To serve, present the bird on a warm plate whole and carve it if it is large (p. 12), or joint it (pp. 20,28). Serve the gravy separately.

When cooking a roast chicken, wash and dry the bird and season with spices and herbs. Place it on a rack in a roasting pan. This corn-fed free-range chicken will be basted with chicken stock as it cooks, as for Roast Chicken, French Style (p. 12).

When stuffing birds, allow extra cooking time for the stuffing to cook through. Always wait till you are about to cook a bird before stuffing it. Either sew up the cavity or close it with small skewers. See Roast Stuffed Chicken with Cheese (p. 14) for an alternative stuffing method.

Roast Chicken

Use this old-fashioned method of roasting for stuffed roast chicken as well. There are recipes for the stuffing on pages 14, 15 and 17 Serve with gravy and roast vegetables.

1 chicken	1 tablespoon olive oil
Pepper	1 tablespoon olive oil
2 garlic cloves	GRAVY
3 thyme sprigs	350 ml/12 fl oz/1½ cups chicken stock (p. 44)
30 g/1 oz/2 tablespoons butter	1 tablespoon flour

Prepare the chicken according to the instructions on page 10. Put some pepper and the garlic, thyme and a little of the butter inside the cavity. Rub the rest of the butter over the chicken with the olive oil. Place the chicken on its side on a rack in a roasting pan. Cook in a preheated oven at 220°C/425°F/gas 7 for 20 minutes. Reduce the heat to 200°C/400°F/gas 6, turn the chicken on its other side, baste with the pan juices and roast for 20 minutes. Turn the bird breast side up, baste and roast for 30 minutes or until done (that is, the juice runs clear when pricked). Remove the chicken to a warm place and leave it to rest for 15 minutes while you make the gravy. Salt if liked.
Serves 5-6

Gravy. Pour off most of the fat from the roasting pan and sprinkle the flour evenly over the surface. Place the pan over a medium heat; stir occasionally until the flour begins to brown. Add the stock little by little, stirring continuously to dispel any lumps. Let the stock reduce to thicken. Serve separately with the roast chicken.

Stuffing Poultry

Mix the stuffing ingredients together in a bowl.	Only fill the cavity three-quarters full, as the stuffing will expand.	Close the opening with small skewers or sew up with a large needle and cotton.	Place the chicken on a rack in a roasting pan.

Roast Vegetables—carrots, potatoes, onions, sweet potatoes. Wash, dry and brush the vegetables with oil, pepper and a little thyme. Bake on a rack in the same oven as the chicken for the same length of time. A head of garlic roasted for 30 minutes makes a delicious addition to roast vegetables; the cloves will just pop out of the skins.

Carving a Large Chicken or Turkey

| Carve one side of the bird, then repeat the process on the other side. First remove the wishbone. | Cut off the legs at the point where the thigh joins the main body. | Slice the meat from the legs. | Carve the breast in vertical slices starting halfway down the breast. Remove the wing. |

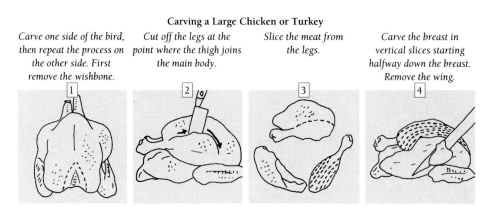

Roast Chicken, French Style

This is a healthy and foolproof way of obtaining a moist, succulent chicken. The stock in the pan steams the chicken underneath and keeps it moist while the skin on top bakes crisp. The sauce is thickened by reduction, rather than with flour.

1 chicken	45 g/1½ oz/3 tablespoons butter
1 teaspoon pepper	Juice of 1 lemon
Small bunch of tarragon or 1 tablespoon dry	350 ml/12 fl oz/1½ cups chicken stock (p. 44)
tarragon	250 ml/8 fl oz/1 cup white wine

Prepare the chicken (p. 10) and put the pepper, tarragon and a little of the butter in the cavity. Rub the butter and lemon juice all over the skin; sprinkle with pepper. Put the chicken, breast side up, on a rack in a roasting pan, and pour the chicken stock into the pan. Place in a preheated oven at 220°C/425°F/gas 7. Baste every 15 minutes with the stock in the pan. After 20 minutes reduce the heat to 200°C/400°F gas 6. Add water to the stock if it begins to dry up. The chicken should be ready in 1¼ hours or when the juice runs free. Salt if liked. Transfer the chicken to a warm place.
Serves 5-6

Roast Chicken, French Style, cooked with whole heads of garlic and seasoned with thyme. Tarragon and rosemary also make for delicious, aromatic chicken.

French Style Sauce. Sop up the fat from the top of the stock with paper towels or spoon it off. Put the roasting pan over a high heat, add the wine and reduce the sauce to about 250 ml/8 fl oz/ 1 cup. Strain into a sauce-boat.

Variation: Add 125 ml/4 fl oz/1/2 cup of single (light) cream instead of the wine after you have reduced the stock.

Making a Fat-Free Sauce from Pan Juices. Strain the juices from the pan after you have scraped the bottom to lift up any sediment. Spoon off the fat that rises to the top and then lift off the rest with paper towels. There is a sauce-boat which is excellent and does this for you. It has two spouts; one pours from the top, taking off the fat, and the other pours from the bottom—fat-free sauce.

Roast Stuffed Chicken with Cheese

This way of stuffing a chicken ensures that plenty of flavour develops between the skin and the flesh. Although it doesn't look as good as a neatly trussed chicken, I believe it is tastier.

1 chicken	60 g/2 oz/1 cup basil, finely chopped
225 g/8 oz/1 cup fresh soft cheese	Pepper
3 tablespoons milk	350 ml/12 fl oz/1½ cups chicken stock (p. 44)
1 cup parsley, finely chopped	Salt

After preparing the chicken (p. 10), gently put your fingers between the skin and the flesh of the chicken and prise it apart all along the breasts and thighs.

Prepare the stuffing by mixing the cheese, milk, herbs and pepper in a food processor. Push the mixture into the pockets you have formed in the chicken. Close up the openings around the neck cavity with skewers. Place the chicken on a rack in a roasting pan and pour in the stock.

Roast in a preheated oven at 220°C/425°F/gas 7 for 20 minutes, then reduce the temperature to 200°C/400°F/gas 6 for another 50 minutes or until cooked. Baste with pan juices every 15 minutes. Leave to rest in a warm place for 15 minutes. Strain the excess fat off the pan juices and serve the juices with the chicken.

Serves 4

Cleaning a Duck. Trim the duck of any extraneous fat, inside and outside. Be sure to pull out the loose fat around the neck and cavity. Press the two little oil glands near the base of the tail to empty them. Wash the duck under cold running water. Pat dry with paper towels. Prick the duck all over with a skewer to release the fat while it cooks.

Roast Duck with Sage and Onion Stuffing served with a reduction sauce made from the pan juices.

Roast Duck with Sage and Onion Stuffing

An old-fashioned English dish that is hard to beat. Make the sauce the same way as for Roast Chicken, French Style (p. 12). You can also vary this dish by using the roast turkey stuffing on page 17.

STUFFING
30 g/1 oz/2 tablespoons butter
1 large onion, chopped
125 g/4 oz/2 cups fresh breadcrumbs
10 sage leaves, chopped
Peel and juice of 1 lemon
1 egg, lightly beaten
Pepper

1.75 kg/3¾ lb duck
30 g/1 oz/2 tablespoons butter
Stock
Duck giblets
250 ml/8 fl oz/1 cup water
250 ml/8 fl oz/1 cup red wine
1 onion, chopped
1 carrot, chopped
Salt and pepper

To make the stuffing: Melt the butter and add the chopped onion. Cook until the onion is translucent and golden, then transfer the onion and butter to a bowl and add the other stuffing ingredients. Mix well.

Prepare the duck as in 'Cleaning a Duck' (p. 14). Stuff the duck and close the neck by sewing or with skewers. Place on a rack in a roasting pan. Rub the butter over the duck. Put all the stock ingredients into the pan. Place in a preheated oven at 220°C/425°F/gas 7 and roast for 15 minutes, then reduce the temperature to 190°C/375°F/gas 5 and cook for a further 1½ hours.

Remove the duck to a warm place. Strain the pan juices after scooping off the fat. Return the juices to the roasting pan and over a high heat reduce the sauce to about 250 ml/8 fl oz/1 cup; serve in a sauce-boat.

Serves 4

Carving a Large Duck

| *Remove the wishbone.* | *Put the bird on its breast and cut through the legs, severing the ball joint. Cut the leg in two.* | *Turn the duck breast side up and carve the breast in vertical slices.* | *Repeat for the other side.* |

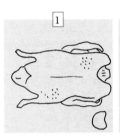
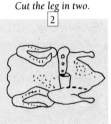

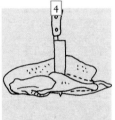

Stuffed Roast Turkey with Apricot Sauce

Turkey meat can be very dry, so the aim of this method of roasting turkey is to keep the meat as moist as possible. Large pieces of pork belly skin tied over the breast and thighs of the turkey not only keep the bird moist but baste it at the same time, which can be difficult otherwise with such a large, heavy bird.

APPLE AND PRUNE STUFFING

2 onions, chopped

15 g/½ oz/1 tablespoon butter

125 g/4 oz/2 cups fresh breadcrumbs

125 g/4 oz/1 cup chopped celery

2 apples, chopped

125 g/4 oz/⅔ cup soaked pitted prunes, chopped

60 g/2 oz/½ cup Brazil nuts

2 tablespoons chopped rosemary

2 tablespoons chopped parsley

1 tablespoon cinnamon

2 eggs

1 turkey

Pork belly skin with fat

Pepper

Rosemary sprigs

APRICOT SAUCE

225 g/8 oz/1¾ cups dried apricots, soaked

125 g/4 oz/½ cup caster (superfine) sugar

1 cinnamon stick

2 teaspoons lemon juice

Brandy, optional

To make the stuffing, cook the onions in the butter until translucent, put them into a bowl with the rest of the stuffing ingredients and mix well.

Wash and dry the turkey. Pack both ends with the stuffing and sew up the openings. Gently rub pepper over the skin and under the skin. Put rosemary sprigs under the skin and tie some on top and under the legs and wings. Place the pork skin all over the turkey and tie it in place with string. Place the turkey in a baking dish and pour in 2.5 cm/1 inch of water, which also helps to keep a dry bird moist. This way the turkey roasts and steams simultaneously.

Place the turkey in a preheated oven at 160°C/325°F/gas 3.

Cooking time: birds under 7 kg/16 lb, 40 minutes to the kilogram/20 minutes to the pound; birds over 7 kg/15 lb, 30 minutes to the kilogram/15 minutes to the pound.

Serves: A 3–4 kg (6–9 lb) turkey will serve 8–10 people. A 4–7 kg (9–16 lb) turkey will serve 10 to 16 people. A 7–9 kg (16–20 lb) turkey will serve 16 to 18 people.

Test for doneness the same way as for chicken (p. 10). Leave the turkey to rest in a warm place for 20 minutes before serving. Meanwhile, make the sauce.

Apricot Sauce. Put all the ingredients into a saucepan, bring to the boil and simmer until the apricots are soft. Remove the cinnamon stick and blend the sauce in the food processor. Add a tablespoon or two of brandy at the end if liked.

Left: The stuffing ingredients ready for Roast Duck with Sage and Onion Stuffing. Stuff the duck just before cooking in order to prevent any harmful bacteria developing.

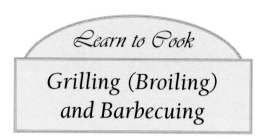

Grilling (Broiling) and Barbecuing

Simple grilled or broiled chicken pieces with crisp skin and juicy meat make a succulent and quickly made meal. One of the most important things to remember is to cook under a preheated grill (broiler) at moderate heat so that the meat doesn't dry out before the chicken is cooked through. The heat source should be 12.5–15 cm/5–6 inches away from the chicken.

If you have the time, marinate the meat for several hours to make it nice and moist. Even 30 minutes is better than not at all.

Frequently baste the meat with a marinade while it is cooking. Basting helps to sear and brown the outside and seals in the juices. Always put the marinade on with a brush.

Turn the chicken pieces once only while cooking. Use tongs; do not pierce the flesh with a fork or you will let valuable juices escape.

Chicken pieces should take about 30–40 minutes to cook, 15–20 minutes each side. Test with a skewer; if the juice runs free, without any pinkness, the chicken is ready.

Turkey and duck pieces can be grilled the same way but may take longer to cook. Prick the duck skin all over before cooking.

When barbecuing, or cooking with the heat source below, poultry pieces can be cooked exactly the same way. Trim meat of fat to prevent flare-ups.

If you are using a ribbed grill, brush it with oil. Place the chicken down carefully each time so that the grid marks form an interesting pattern.

Grilled (Broiled) Chicken

A simple and tasty way to grill or barbecue a chicken. Serve with a salad or grilled tomatoes and crusty bread.

3 tablespoons olive oil
Juice and zest of 1 lemon
2 tablespoons rosemary
2 garlic cloves, finely chopped

1 teaspoon pepper
1 chicken, cut into 6 pieces (p. 20)
4 lemon wedges, as garnish

Mix the oil, lemon, rosemary, garlic and pepper together and marinate the chicken pieces in the mixture for an hour. Place the chicken under an oiled, preheated grill (broiler). Cook for 15 minutes, basting several times. Turn over and cook and baste for a further 15 minutes. Check with a skewer to see if the meat is cooked.

Serves 4

Grilled (Broiled) Chicken flavoured with rosemary and lemon juice makes a delectable Sunday lunch.

Always endeavour to marinate chicken pieces before grillling or barbecuing. It adds flavour and keeps the meat moist while it cooks at a high temperature.

Jointing a Chicken

Cut off the legs at the point where the thigh joins the body.	*Slide a knife inside the chicken and cut each side of the backbone. Remove the backbone.*	*Turn the bird over and cut down one side of the breastbone to divide it in two.*	*Cut off the wing with a piece of the breast from each side. There are now six pieces.*

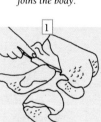 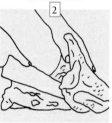  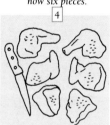

Tandoori Chicken

This tender spiced chicken is cooked whole but split in half and flattened. It is best marinated for an hour or up to 24 hours if you have time–the yoghurt tenderizes the flesh. Serve with rice and salad.

1 chicken	2 chillies, chopped
250 ml/8 fl oz/1 cup plain yoghurt	Juice of 1 lemon
2 garlic cloves, chopped	1 tablespoon garam masala (p. 40)
1 tablespoon chopped ginger	1 teaspoon turmeric

Split the chicken open along the backbone and cut the backbone out with poultry shears. Cut the wing and leg joints enough to flatten them out, and pound the chicken until it is as flat as you can make it without damaging the flesh. Remove the skin if you wish.

Mix the other ingredients together. Marinate the split chicken in the mixture for 1 to 3 hours. Put the chicken under a preheated grill (broiler) for 15 minutes, turn, baste, and cook for a further 15 minutes. Cook for another 5 minutes on both sides, basting, and test for doneness. Cut into 4 pieces to serve on a bed of rice.

Serves 4

Splitting a Chicken

A whole chicken is split in half by cutting along both sides of the backbone. Remove the backbone.   *Flatten the chicken out with your hands and remove the skin.*   *Marinate and grill (broil) the chicken.*   *Cut the chicken into four pieces ready to serve.*

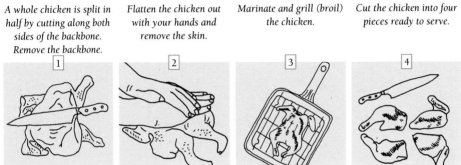

Thai Satay Sticks

Everyone loves satay sticks, whether they be from Thailand, Indonesia, or Malaysia. Serve one as a snack or several as a main meal. They are always served with spicy peanut sauce. Soak the bamboo skewers in water for 30 minutes before using, to prevent them from burning.

MARINADE
2 chillies, chopped
1 small onion, chopped
1 teaspoon laos powder
1 tablespoon chopped ginger
1 tablespoon chopped garlic

1 tablespoon chopped lemon grass
Zest and juice of 1 lemon
3 tablespoons coconut milk (p. 40)
1 tablespoon soy sauce

4 chicken breasts, cut into 18 mm/³⁄₄ inch cubes

Combine all the marinade ingredients in a food processor and blend to a smooth paste. Marinate the chicken for 2 hours, then thread the pieces onto skewers. Grill as on page 18, basting often. They should need only 5 minutes on either side. Serve immediately with salad and Peanut Sauce (next page).

Serves 4-6

Peanut Sauce. Make your sauce thick and crunchy or fine and smooth—blend the peanuts according to preference. Use unsalted peanut butter if you are in a hurry.

275 g/10 oz/2 cups shelled, skinned raw peanuts
   (groundnuts)
2 tablespoons oil
1 small onion, thinly sliced
2 garlic cloves, chopped

4 chillies, chopped
250 ml/8 fl oz/1 cup water
½ teaspoon sugar
1 teaspoon salt
2 tablespoons lemon juice

Grind the peanuts in a food processor. Heat the oil and cook the onion until translucent. Add the garlic and chillies and cook for a minute, then pour in the water, peanuts, sugar and salt. Stir and simmer until the sauce is smooth and thick, then stir in the lemon juice.

Poussin (Spatchcock) or Quail with Mustard

A delightful way to cook smaller birds. Poussins are very small chickens. Use one poussin or two quails per serving. Serve with large grilled (broiled) mushrooms and tomatoes.

4 poussins or 8 quails
MARINADE
1 tablespoon olive oil
30 g/1 oz/2 tablespoons butter, melted

1 teaspoon pepper
2 tablespoons French mustard
2 tablespoons finely chopped tarragon
1 tablespoon finely chopped parsley

Split the poussins or quails as for Tandoori Chicken (p. 20). Mix all the marinade ingredients together and brush over the birds. Cook under a preheated grill (broiler) as described on page 18. Turn after 10 minutes and baste frequently. Poussins should take 30–40 minutes, quails 20–30 minutes. Pour the pan juices over the birds and serve with steaming rice.
Serves 4

Clarified Butter. *Clarified butter is pure butterfat with the milk solids and impurities removed. This allows the butter to reach a high temperature when cooked without burning, which is necessary when frying or sautéing. You can make up the quantity suggested and store it in the refrigerator until needed. It lasts indefinitely.*

Melt 225 g/8 oz/1 cup unsalted butter gently and allow it to simmer but not burn. It is ready when the top is clear and the solids are on the bottom. Remove from heat, rest until warm, and strain the clear yellow liquid into bowl through a layer of muslin (cheesecloth) in a fine sieve. Chill.

Variation: *Clarify leftover fat from a roast duck or goose the same way, to remove any impurities. Duck fat is wonderful to use for sautéing potatoes and to make hearty winter casseroles.*

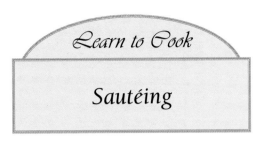

Learn to Cook

Sautéing

Sauté means to brown and cook food quickly in a small quantity of very hot oil, or a mixture of oil and butter, in a large frying pan (skillet). Butter alone, unless clarified, will burn.

Chicken pieces are browned evenly until tender and can then be simmered in just enough liquid to cover—wine, water or stock. Vegetables can be added for colour and flavour. It is a simple cooking technique that will make a dish in 30 minutes.

When sautéing, make sure the oil or oil and butter combination is very hot, otherwise there will be no browning and the juices will not be sealed in.

It is essential to dry the chicken pieces first, since dampness causes steam which prevents the browning and sealing process.

The pan must not be crowded. Allow space between the chicken pieces, otherwise the chicken will steam rather than brown, causing juices to escape and burn the pan.

Sautéing a Chicken

| *Wash and dry the chicken pieces thoroughly.* | *The oil and butter should be very hot before adding the chicken.* | *Sauté the chicken pieces in an uncrowded pan until golden brown.* | *Pour in liquid to just cover the chicken, and simmer until cooked.* |

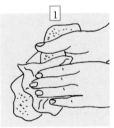   

Before beginning a recipe, read it through thoroughly and check the ingredients and the time it will take to make. Prepare the ingredients beforehand for quick-cooking dishes like Chicken Sauté.

Chicken Sauté Provençale

Serve this flavoursome dish with steamed rice. Add some olives a few minutes before serving, if liked.

1 chicken, cut into 6 pieces (p. 20)
1 teaspoon pepper
2 tablespoons oil
30 g/1 oz/2 tablespoons butter
2 garlic cloves, finely chopped
2 onions, sliced

2 large green peppers (capsicums, bell peppers),
  seeded and sliced
250 ml/8 fl oz/1 cup white wine
2 large tomatoes, chopped
1 tablespoon chopped oregano or basil
Salt

Dry the chicken pieces and season lightly with pepper. Heat the oil and butter in a large frying pan (skillet) over a high heat. When foaming subsides, add as many chicken pieces, skin side down, as can fit comfortably in one layer. Sauté for 2–3 minutes on both sides, using tongs to turn them. Remove to a warm plate.

Add the garlic, onions and peppers to the pan, and cook over a low heat, stirring occasionally, until they soften. Return the chicken pieces to the pan and add the wine, tomatoes and herbs. Bring to the boil, cover and simmer for 30 minutes or until the chicken is tender. Taste and adjust the seasoning if necessary.

Serves 6

Turkey Escalopes

Cut four thin, even slices from a turkey breast or buy them as escalopes. This is a rich, succulent dish, so serve it with a green salad and some fresh buttered noodles.

3 tablespoons flour
1 teaspoon pepper
1 teaspoon thyme
4 turkey escalopes
60 g/2 oz/¼ cup butter

1 tablespoon olive oil
4 slices Parma ham (prosciutto)
4 thin slices Gruyére cheese
5 tablespoons white wine

Flour and season the escalopes (see 'Dredging with Flour', p. 35). Coat the escalopes evenly with the flour. Melt the butter and oil in a large frying pan (skillet); when hot, cook the escalopes over a moderate heat for 5 minutes on each side. Quickly place a slice of ham on top of each escalope, followed by a slice of cheese. Pour the wine over, cover the pan and cook over a low heat for 10 minutes. Serve on a warm plate with the pan juices.

Serves 4

Previous pages: Chicken Fillets with Mushrooms (p. 30) make a delectable lunch or supper dish.
Right: Flavoursome Chicken Sauté Provençale ready to serve to guests. The chicken is sautéed until golden brown and then simmered in wine until tender.

Deglazed Pan Sauce. *To make a tasty pan sauce, 'deglaze' the pan. In other words, lift the delicious sediment from the bottom of the pan with liquid, such as wine, stock or cream. Then reduce the liquid to a sauce consistency. Stir constantly to mix the flavour of the sediment and the liquid. Keep your cooked poultry in a warm place while you make the sauce.*

Jointing a Duck

| *Cut out the wishbone.* | *Turn the duck onto its breast and cut down either side of the backbone. Discard it.* | *Cut out the breast and cut in half. Cut the leg and wing section in half.* | *There are now six pieces.* |

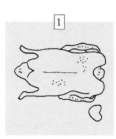 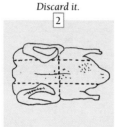  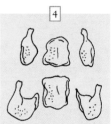

Duck Breasts with Balsamic Vinegar and Grapes

If grapes are out of season you can use sultanas (golden raisins) previously soaked in water and drained. Use this recipe for cooking whole quails as well, they need 10 minutes less cooking time overall.

1 tablespoon olive oil	1 teaspoon pepper
4 duck breasts, skin pricked	6 juniper berries
1–2 tablespoons balsamic vinegar	30 small seedless grapes, stalks removed

Heat the oil and put the duck breasts in, skin side down. Cook for 5 minutes on each side. Add the rest of the ingredients. Cover and cook for 15 minutes or until the duck is tender. Spoon or pour the excess fat off the sauce and pour over the duck breasts to serve.
Serves 4

Thawing Poultry. *You must thaw any poultry thoroughly before cooking; otherwise you may be preserving harmful bacteria that won't be killed off in the cooking process. Check inside the cavity that the bones are not still frozen. It is best to thaw slowly in the refrigerator. If it needs to be done faster, thaw at room temperature. Cook immediately the poultry is thawed. Chicken will take 24 hours to thaw in the refrigerator, turkey and goose 48 hours, duck 24 hours, poussin 12 hours, guinea-fowl 24 hours.*

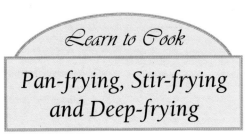

Learn to Cook

Pan-frying, Stir-frying and Deep-frying

Pan-frying is a delicious and fast way to cook chicken with the minimum amount of fat. Always use a frying pan (skillet) just a little larger than the chicken pieces, otherwise the surrounding fat will burn. Don't crowd the pieces together or they will steam. Use a good cold-pressed olive oil or a combination of oil and butter, because butter alone will burn unless it is clarified (p. 22). Seal the surfaces first, to enclose the juices, cooking the first side a little longer. Add salt only after the chicken is cooked, otherwise it will draw the juices out. Make sure the pan and fat are very hot before putting the chicken in. Dry the chicken pieces or the juice may create steam. Don't use large pieces of chicken, as they will take too long to cook.

Stir-frying in a wok is a very fast and healthy way to cook chicken. The wok has a large heating surface, which enables you to seal the poultry very fast and so retain the juices. The ingredients must be bite-sized pieces. Have all ingredients prepared ready beside the wok, including the flavourings, as you must work fast to achieve crisp but cooked stir-fry dishes. The wok should be very hot before adding oil and food. You must stir the food constantly so that it doesn't over cook on one side or begin steaming.

Deep-frying is not as popular as it used to be, because it adds too much fat to the food, so we recommend cooking this way just occasionally. Always use very clean oil, preferably peanut (groundnut) oil, as it does not burn easily at high temperatures. The oil should be very hot so that the food absorbs the minimum of fat and seals the meat quickly—about 180°C/350°F. Use a large, deep saucepan, only one-third filled with oil in case it bubbles up when food is added. Dry the food before cooking, or coat it in batter, flour or egg and breadcrumbs. Fry small amounts at a time, or the food will reduce the temperature of the oil. Don't fry large pieces of poultry, as they take too long to cook and so absorb too much fat.

Stir-frying

Velvet the chicken.	*Prepare all the ingredients before beginning to cook and place them near the wok.*	*Heat the wok and then heat the oil until it is very hot.*	*Stir the food continuously until the dish is completed.*

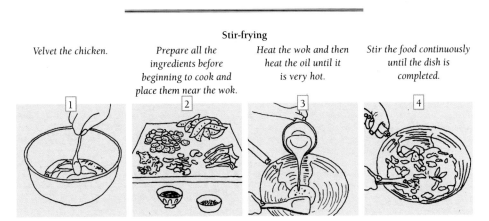

Chicken Fillets with Mushrooms

This is a delicious and fast pan-fry dish. Chicken fillets are skinless, boneless half-breasts. You can use grapes or asparagus as an alternative to mushrooms, add them with the cream towards the end of cooking.

8 chicken fillets
30 g/1 oz/2 tablespoons butter
1 tablespoon olive oil
200 g/7 oz mushrooms, wiped and thinly sliced

6 tablespoons chicken stock (p. 44)
Salt and pepper
200 ml/7 fl oz/¾ cup single (light) cream

Remove any tendons from the centre of the chicken fillets very carefully sliding the knife along the tendon so as not to split the fillet. Flatten the fillet slightly to even the thickness. Heat the butter and oil and fry the chicken for 1 minute, then turn. Continue to cook until the chicken is golden and the juice runs clear when pricked. Remove the chicken to a warm place.

Add the mushrooms to the pan and cook in the leftover fat. Deglaze (p. 28) the pan with the chicken stock and stir well. Season with salt and pepper. Reduce the sauce a little, then pour in the cream and cook until it thickens. Serve the chicken fillets surrounded by the mushroom sauce on individual warm plates.

Serves 8

When flattening out a chicken fillet, place it between two sheets of clingfilm (plastic wrap) or greased paper and roll it carefully with a rolling pin. A boning knife is useful to ease the chicken fillet from the breastbone.

Chicken Schnitzels make a delicious light meal with asparagus and a squeeze of lemon. Anchovy fillets or chopped hard-boiled egg and parsley also make a flavoursome garnish for a change.

Chicken Schnitzels

The chicken fillets are coated with breadcrumbs and quickly pan-fried just like real schnitzels. Serve with sauté potatoes and salad.

4 chicken fillets

1 egg, beaten

Pepper

125 g/4 oz/1 cup dried breadcrumbs

60 g/2 oz/¼ cup butter

1 tablespoon oil

4 lemon wedges as garnish

1 tablespoon capers as garnish

Place the fillets between two pieces of clingfilm (plastic wrap) and flatten the chicken with a rolling pin. Trim to a neat shape. Season the egg with pepper and have it in a shallow bowl beside a similar bowl containing the breadcrumbs. Heat the butter and oil in a large pan. Dip the schnitzels in the egg and then in the breadcrumbs and put them straight into the hot fat. Cook for 2–3 minutes on each side until golden brown. Serve on a warm plate and garnish with lemon wedges and capers.

Serves 4

All the ingredients for Stir-Fried Chicken with Walnuts set out ready for cooking. Part of the pleasure of cooking is looking at the beautiful ingredients and their changing appearance in preparation.

Southern Deep-Fried Chicken

Serve with chips (French fries) and coleslaw for the real old-fashioned taste of fried chicken–you'll never want to eat take-away again.

MARINADE
2 tablespoons olive oil
2 tablespoons lemon juice
1 teaspoon pepper
¼ teaspoon cayenne
1 teaspoon chopped oregano

1 chicken, cut into 10 pieces
Flour for coating
Peanut (groundnut) oil for deep-frying
1 egg, beaten
10 lemon wedges as garnish

Combine the marinade ingredients and marinate the chicken for an hour or more, turning occasionally. Pat dry the chicken and coat with flour. Heat the oil in a deep saucepan. When it is so hot that a bread cube turns golden brown in a minute, put in half the chicken pieces. Cook until golden brown and the juice runs clear when pricked. Remove with a slotted spoon; keep warm while you cook the other pieces. Drain on paper towels. Serve with lemon wedges.

Serves 5

Stir-Fried Chicken with Walnuts

Most of the work in Chinese cooking goes into the preparation of the ingredients, so don't let the length of this recipe deter you. 'Velveting' makes the chicken white and fluffy and helps to prevent it from drying out in the cooking process. Serve with steamed rice.

2 chicken breasts, cut into 12 mm/½ inch cubes
1 tablespoon dry sherry
1 egg white
1 tablespoon cornflour (cornstarch)
5 tablespoons oil
45 g/1½ oz/½ cup walnut halves
2 teaspoons cornflour (cornstarch)
1 teaspoon sesame oil

1 tablespoon ginger slices
2 garlic cloves, chopped
2 cups cubed green peppers (capsicums, bell peppers)
125 ml/4 fl oz/½ cup chicken stock (p. 44)
2 tablespoons dry sherry
2 tablespoons light soy sauce

First velvet the chicken. Put the cubes in a bowl and add the sherry and stir. Beat the egg white a few times and add this to the bowl along with the cornflour and 1 tablespoon of oil. Mix well and stir until smooth. Leave to marinate for 30 minutes to 1 hour in the refrigerator.

Heat 2 tablespoons of oil in a wok until hot. Stir in the chicken pieces. Lower the heat and keep stirfrying until the chicken turns white. This process will only take a minute or two. Remove the chicken and strain. Reserve the oil. Do not put the chicken in the refrigerator.

Add the remaining oil to the wok and heat. Put in the walnuts and stir for 1–2 minutes. Take out with a slotted spoon and drain.

Dissolve the cornflour in a little water and add the sesame oil. Heat the wok again and throw in the ginger and garlic, stir, and add the peppers. Keep stir-frying and add the stock. Cover and cook for 2 minutes. Remove the cover, add the chicken, sherry, soy and cornflour. Stir-fry until the liquid makes a smooth sauce and all is lightly cooked but still crisp. Put onto a warm plate with the walnuts on top.

Serves 2-3

Cutting a Small Chicken with Poultry Shears

Wash and dry the chicken.

With the chicken on its breast, cut down either side of the backbone. Discard the backbone.

Open the chicken out flat. Cut off the thigh and leg in one piece.

Trim the breast with the wing attached. There are now four pieces.

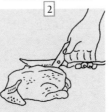

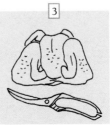

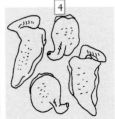

Learn to Cook

Casseroles and Braised Dishes

asseroles—call them ragouts or stews as you please—are toothsome concoctions of bite-sized pieces simmered in their own juices at a low heat and flavoured with mixtures of vegetables and herbs. Braising is the technique of cooking large cuts or whole birds in enough liquid to partially cover them, flavoured and cooked the same way as casseroles—long, slow simmering in a heavy pot, tightly covered so that the food slowly cooks and steams.

Casseroles and braised dishes provide an opportunity to use mature poultry, if you can get them, or any bird you think may be tough or dry.

Cook them either over direct heat or in a slow oven.

A heavy-based, enamelled cast-iron pot with a tight-fitting lid gives the best results. When cooking a whole bird, the pot should be only a bit bigger than the bird.

The meat may be browned lightly first. See 'Sautéing' (pp. 23, 26) for browning technique.

Flour can be added at browning stage to thicken the sauce.

Water, stock, wine, beer, yoghurt or coconut milk are some of the liquids used in these dishes, which are also enhanced by herbs, spices, vegetables, garlic, ginger, shallots, tomatoes and onions.

Once the liquid comes to the boil, cover the pot tightly and simmer until tender.

If the sauce is too thin at the end of cooking, remove the solid food and keep it in a warm place while you reduce the sauce until it thickens.

Coq au vin

The well-known French dish of chicken cooked in red wine with onions and mushrooms. As it is usual to drink the same wine with the dish as that used in the cooking, be generous with the quality of the wine–it is there to enhance the flavour. Serve with mashed potatoes and turnips to soak up the delicious sauce.

60 g/2 oz/2¼ cups butter
1 tablespoon oil
2 bacon rashers (slices), rind removed, cut into
　bite-sized pieces
Flour for dusting
1 chicken, cut into 6 pieces
3 garlic cloves

Bouquet garni (p. 36)
½ bottle red wine
1 teaspoon pepper
18 small pickling (baby) onions, peeled
2 teaspoons sugar
18 button mushrooms, wiped

Heat half the butter and oil in a pot and add the bacon. Put the flour in a paper bag and coat the chicken pieces (see 'Dredging with Flour', p. 35), then place them in the fat and sauté until golden brown. Add the garlic, bouquet garni, red wine and pepper. Stir. When the liquid has come to the boil, either turn the heat down, cover and simmer for about an hour until tender, or put the covered pot in a preheated oven at 180°C/350°F/gas 4.

Meanwhile, boil the whole onions in water until cooked; drain. Heat the remaining oil and butter and add the onions. Sprinkle with sugar and sauté until they are caramelized—that is, when they begin to brown. Remove with a slotted spoon. Sauté the mushrooms in the same fat until they are tender. Ten minutes before serving time, add the onions and mushrooms to the casserole and stir. If your sauce is too thin, you can remove all the solid ingredients and reduce the sauce until it thickens.

Serves 4-6

Dredging with Flour. *The easiest and cleanest way to dust pieces of poultry with flour is to put flour and seasonings into a paper bag, put the pieces in a few at a time, clutch the top of the bag closed, and shake. The pieces will be evenly coated in flour and your kitchen will still be spotless.*

Chicken with Cream Sauce

Serve this rich, luxurious dish with tiny steamed potatoes and carrots.

75 g/2½ oz/5 tablespoons butter
2 bacon rashers (slices), rind removed, diced
1 onion, chopped
1 chicken, cut into 6 pieces
1½ teaspoons pepper
4 tablespoons brandy

Bouquet garni, with carrot (p. 36)
2 tarragon stalks
300 ml/½ pint/1¼ cups cider
125 ml/4 fl oz/½ cup single (light) cream
2 egg yolks

Heat the butter and bacon in a pot and add the onion. Sauté until the onion is translucent, then sauté the chicken pieces until they are golden brown. Remove from the heat and season. Warm the brandy in a small saucepan. Set it alight and pour it flaming over the chicken. This technique adds an extra dimension of flavour to this delicious casserole. Just be careful when setting the brandy alight.

Add the bouquet garni, tarragon and cider. Bring to the boil and then either simmer on the cooker or transfer to a preheated oven at 180°C/350°F/gas 4. Cover tightly. The chicken should be tender in about an hour.

Serves 4-6

Cream sauce. Remove the chicken with a slotted spoon and keep it in a warm place. Strain the cooking liquid into a saucepan. Beat together the cream and egg yolks and mix into the cooking liquid. Cook over a gentle heat until it thickens. Pour the sauce over the chicken pieces.

Braised Whole Chicken

The chicken is roasted in a pot sitting on a bed of herbs and vegetables.

Bouquet garni (see below)
1 chicken, trimmed, washed and dried
1 tablespoon olive oil
90 g/3 oz /6 tablespoons butter
1 celery stick, chopped

1 onion, chopped
1 carrot, chopped
4 tarragon sprigs
250 ml/8 fl oz/1 cup white wine

Put the bouquet garni into the cavity of the chicken. Heat the oil and butter in a casserole pot and brown the chicken all over. Remove the chicken and sweat the vegetables in the same fat for 10 minutes. Place the chicken back in the pot on top of the vegetables. Add the tarragon and the wine and bring the liquid to the boil. Turn the heat down as low as it will go, cover tightly and simmer for about an hour until tender. Remove the chicken to a warm plate, strain the juices into a bowl and lift off the fat. Serve as a sauce with the chicken. You could thicken it with cream and egg yolk as in the previous recipe or add more wine and reduce to thicken.
Serves 4-6

Meal in a Pot. Cook some large pieces of vegetables in the casserole as above and serve the chicken surrounded by them with the sauce separately.

EXTRA INGREDIENTS
6 carrots, cut into thirds
250 ml/8 fl oz/1 cup white wine

12 baby potatoes, skin left on
12 tiny pickling onions

Sit the browned chicken on the bed of sweated chopped vegetables as in the main recipe. Surround the chicken with the extra carrots. Pour over the double quantity of wine and continue cooking as above. Twenty minutes before the end, add the potatoes and onions.
Serves 4-6

> **Bouquet Garni.** *A bouquet garni is a small bunch of herbs, preferably fresh, which is used to flavour stews and braised and boiled dishes. Take several twigs of thyme, a bay leaf and several stalks of parsley, and tie the bouquet with string. If you only have dried leaves, enclose the leaves in a small muslin (cheesecloth) bag and tie with string. You can also add dried orange peel, lavender, or a stick of carrot if liked.*

A portion of Braised Whole Chicken served with a sauce thickened with cream and egg yolk. Mangetout (snow peas) and steamed potatoes complete this delicious family meal.

Guinea-Fowl with Cabbage

A favourite German way to cook guinea-fowl. This method ensures a moist, succulent bird. You'll be delighted with the taste of the cabbage cooked this way.

½ cabbage, cut into 4 wedges
1 large carrot, cut into 4 and halved lengthwise
60 g/2 oz/¼ cup butter
2 bacon rashers (slices), rind removed, cut into
    bite-sized pieces
1 onion, chopped
1 guinea-fowl, halved

3 pork sausages, cut into bite-sized pieces
125 ml/4 fl oz/½ cup white wine
125 ml/4 fl oz/½ cup chicken stock (p. 44)
Bouquet garni (p. 36)
1 teaspoon pepper
6 juniper berries

Blanch the cabbage and carrot in boiling water for 10 minutes. Melt the butter in casserole pot. Add the bacon and onion and cook until the onion is translucent. Add the guinea-fowl and sauté until golden brown. Remove the fowl and place the cabbage and carrot on top of the bacon and onion. Add the guinea-fowl skin side up. Surround with the sausages and pour in the wine and stock; add the bouquet garni, pepper and juniper berries. Bring the liquid to the boil, turn down the heat as low as it will go, cover tightly and simmer for about 1 1/4 hours or until the guinea-fowl is tender. Remove the solid ingredients to a warm plate. Reduce the sauce until it thickens. Strain and remove the fat. Serve separately.

Serves 4

Spicy Chicken on a bed of Coriander (Cilantro)

This curry comes from India and is cooked in the same way as the previous casseroles except that the chicken pieces are not browned to begin with. Serve with steamed turmeric rice. You can remove the chicken skin for this dish to make it a perfect meal for a low-fat diet.

2 onions, quartered
4 garlic cloves
1 tablespoon chopped ginger
3 chillies, chopped
75 g/2½ oz/1 packed cup chopped coriander
    (cilantro)
Juice of 1 lemon
1 tablespoon oil

1 teaspoon turmeric
1 teaspoon ground cardamom seeds
1 tablespoon garam masala (p. 44)
250 ml/8 fl oz/1 cup low-fat plain yoghurt
2 tomatoes, diced
1 chicken, cut into 6 pieces
Coriander leaves to garnish

Braised poultry is browned first in oil or an oil-and-butter combination and then placed on a sweated bed of vegetables and herbs. Wine, beer, water or stock is poured in halfway up the depth of the bird so that the bird will simmer and steam slowly and remain moist.

Put the onions, garlic, ginger, chillies, coriander and lemon into a food processor and blend to a paste. Heat the oil in a casserole pot and add the turmeric, cardamom and garam masala. Stir for several minutes, then add the paste. Cook for 5 minutes, and add the yoghurt and tomatoes. Stir and cook for a further 5 minutes, then add the chicken pieces. Turn the pieces until they are coated with the spicy paste. Turn the heat down low, cover tightly and simmer for an hour. You can reduce the sauce if necessary. Garnish with coriander leaves.
Serves 4-6

Variation. Use 250 ml/8 fl oz/1 cup of coconut milk (see below) instead of yoghurt and mint or basil instead of coriander.

Garam Masala

Homemade garam masala is far superior to the bought product. If you use good ingredients to start with and keep the spice in an airtight jar in the refrigerator, it will last for months.

1 tablespoon cardamom seeds	*1 teaspoon peppercorns*
1 tablespoon cumin seeds	*1 nutmeg*
1 teaspoon cloves	*1 cinnamon stick*

Grind the spices together in a clean coffee grinder or food mill or with a mortar and pestle. Store in a screw-topped jar in the refrigerator.

Coconut Milk. *You can make coconut milk from freshly grated coconut and freeze the leftover grated coconut or milk if the whole quantity isn't required. Preparing your own makes an amazing difference to the taste of Asian food, and it is not hard work if you make a large quantity ready for the next few dishes.*

When buying a coconut, shake it to make sure it has plenty of liquid in it and is therefore fresh. Crack it in half. (The liquid isn't used except for a drink.) Prise the coconut flesh from the skin and wash. Shred the flesh in a food processor. Freeze what isn't required for the immediate recipe.

150 g/5 oz/3 cups shredded coconut
300 ml/½ pint/1¼ cups boiling water

Pour the water over the coconut and leave to stand for 5 minutes. Strain it through a piece of muslin (cheesecloth) lining a sieve. Press well to squeeze out all the liquid. This is known as thick coconut milk. Makes 1½ cups.
For thin coconut milk, repeat the process twice using the pulp left from the thick coconut milk.

Boiling
and Poaching

Boiled meats are simmered slowly with vegetables in a large pot of water—an ancient way of cooking the entire meal over a fire. The only thing you must have is time. You are also left with a pot of delicious stock. Just boil it down to intensify the flavour.

The richer the boiling liquid, the better the meat will taste, so when boiling a chicken start if possible with some of your already made frozen stock or add some pig's trotters, hocks or veal bones to the water.

Never boil a chicken quickly; it should be just a gentle simmer. Always put the bird into simmering liquid, not cold. Cover to cook, leaving room for the steam to escape.

Skim the surface thoroughly after the liquid comes to the boil.

When poaching a chicken, the liquid—stock or wine—comes halfway up the chicken so that the dark meat boils and the light meat steams. The resulting stock is boiled down to turn into a sauce. Always use a pot just a bit bigger than the chicken, and it should have a tight-fitting lid.

Truss the chicken for boiling and poaching (see the illustration on p. 42.) The chicken may also be stuffed—try the stuffing on page 15 or page 17.

Poule au pot

This literally means chicken in a pot, a dish beloved by good King Henry the Fourth, who wished that every family in France could afford to put a chicken in a pot every Sunday.

STUFFING

3 bacon rashers (slices), rind removed, sliced into matchsticks

1 egg

Salt and pepper

½ teaspoon grated nutmeg

1 tablespoon chopped shallots or onion

2 garlic cloves, chopped

30 g/1 oz/½ cup chopped parsley

2 tablespoons chopped tarragon

125 g/4 oz/2 cups fresh breadcrumbs

1 chicken

4 carrots

4 turnips

2 leeks

2 onions

2 celery sticks

Put all the stuffing ingredients into a bowl and mix well. After washing the chicken and patting it dry, stuff the cavity and sew up or skewer it to close. Truss the chicken (p. 42) and put it into simmering water in a large pot. After 30 minutes add the vegetables. The chicken should take no longer than 1½ hours to cook. Serve with Velouté Sauce or Mayonnaise (p. 46).
Serves 4-6

Velouté Sauce

30 g/1 oz /2 tablespoons butter
1½ tablespoons flour
300 ml/½ pint/1¼ cups chicken stock (p. 44)
Salt and pepper

1 tablespoon lemon juice
1 egg yolk
1 tablespoon single (light) cream
1 tablespoon chopped parsley or chervil

Melt the butter in a saucepan and sprinkle in the flour. Stir for a minute to cook the flour, then remove the pan from the heat. Stir in the stock. Keep stirring until it is smooth, then put it back over a low heat. Stir from time to time until it comes to the boil. Simmer for about 10 minutes and season with salt, pepper and lemon juice.

Mix the egg yolk and cream together and add a little of the sauce. Pour it into the pan and stir until the sauce thickens; remove from heat. Stir in the chopped herb.

Trussing a Chicken

| Stretch the neck flap under the chicken and fold back the wing tips. | Cut out the wishbone. | Tie the leg ends together with string at the neck end. | Tie the wings so that they remain in position under the bird. |

  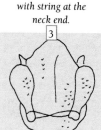 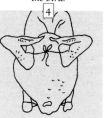

Poached Chicken with Mushroom Stuffing

Serve this with Velouté Sauce (above) or Mayonnaise (p. 46) and steamed vegetables. Jointed pieces also may be cooked this way, though they will take only about 30 minutes to cook.

STUFFING
1 tablespoon chopped shallots or onion
275 g/10 oz/1½ cups cooked rice
2 garlic cloves, chopped
125 g/4 oz mushrooms, quartered
Salt and pepper
2 tablespoons Madeira or port
1 egg
1 tablespoon chopped thyme

1 chicken
30 g/1 oz/2 tablespoons butter
1 carrot, sliced
1 onion, sliced
1 celery stick, sliced
250 ml/8 fl oz/1 cup dry white wine
750 ml/1¼ pints/3 cups hot chicken stock (p. 44)

A really old-fashioned family dish which is excellent for today's light approach to cooking. Poached Chicken with Mushroom Stuffing deserves to be made with a free-range chicken—it makes a meal fit for a god.

Sauté the shallots or onions and then mix all the stuffing ingredients together, stuff the chicken and close the cavity.

Melt the butter in a pot and stir in the carrot, onion and celery. Cook until they soften. Place the chicken in the pot breast side up. Pour in the wine and enough chicken stock so that the liquid comes halfway up the chicken. Bring the stock to the boil, turn the heat down to simmer and cover tightly. The chicken should be done in 1 1/4 hours. Test with a skewer (p. 10). Remove the chicken to a warm place while you make the sauce.

Serves 4-6

Chicken Stock

A good stock is the basis of many dishes and sauces. Keep a ready supply in the freezer. Stocks should simmer for at least 3 hours to extract the maximum flavour. Skim carefully to make the stock clear.

1.25 kg/2½ lb chicken bones and veal bones	2 celery sticks
1 teaspoon peppercorns	Bouquet garni (p. 36)
1 onion	1 teaspoon salt, optional
1 carrot	

Put all the ingredients except the salt into a large saucepan. Pour in just enough water to cover the bones. Bring to the boil slowly and keep skimming the surface to remove all the scum. Simmer gently for 3 hours. Add salt to taste. Strain the stock into a bowl and, when cool, chill. Remove the fat when it has set solid on the surface. Freeze if not required within 5 days.

The poached chicken has just been placed in its bed of vegetables and the wine and chicken stock poured over it until halfway up the chicken.

Chicken Soup

A homely, comforting soup to start a meal or eat as a light meal with crusty bread. Some people claim it can cure all kinds of illness and melancholia.

30 g/1 oz/2 tablespoons butter

1 onion, chopped

3 carrots, cut into dice

2 turnips, cut into dice

2 celery sticks, cut into dice

1.75 litres/3 pints/2 quarts chicken stock (p. 44)

90 g/3 oz/½ cup pearl barley, soaked overnight

2 chicken breasts, cut into bite-sized pieces

1 teaspoon salt

1 teaspoon pepper

2 tablespoons finely chopped parsley, to garnish

Melt the butter in a saucepan and put in the onion. When it begins to turn translucent, add the rest of the vegetables. Stir for 5 minutes to sweat, then pour in the stock and barley. Cover and cook slowly for 20 minutes. Add the chicken meat and season with salt and pepper. Cover and simmer for 10–15 minutes or until the vegetables and chicken are cooked. Garnish with the parsley.

Serves 6

Chinese White Chicken

An Asian way of poaching a chicken to eat cold with sauces or to turn into a chicken salad, chicken noodle soup or sandwiches. You'll be surprised how handy it is to be able to cook a chicken this way and turn it into so many different dishes. Keep the cooking liquid for a light stock.

1 chicken

1 tablespoon sliced ginger

3 spring onions (scallions), chopped

2 garlic cloves

1 tablespoon soy sauce

½ teaspoon pepper

Place the chicken in a pot just a bit bigger than the chicken and pour boiling water over to cover the bird. Add the ginger, onions and garlic. Bring to the boil and then simmer for 10 minutes. Cover and remove from the heat. Leave the chicken to stand in the stock for 4 hours. It will gently cook all the way through and you will find it is deliciously moist and tender. Remove the chicken from the stock and pat dry. Serve cold, cut into portions, or serve with noodles or steamed rice.

Serves 4-6

Coriander Garnish for White Chicken. Sprinkle the chicken pieces with 1 cup of coriander (cilantro) leaves, 4 spring onions cut into finger-length thin shreds, and 2 tablespoons of ginger cut into thin shreds. Mix together 2 teaspoons of sesame oil and 2 tablespoons each of light soy sauce and sherry and pour this over the chicken just before serving.

Waldorf Chicken Salad

Everyone loves chicken salad. It is always the favourite on a buffet table or at a picnic. Cook the chicken as in the previous recipe to get moist and tender meat.

1 Chinese White Chicken (p. 45)
2 celery sticks, chopped
1 apple, diced
60 g/2 oz/½ cup chopped walnuts
Salt and pepper

125 ml/4 fl oz/½ cup soured cream
125 ml/4 fl oz/½ cup mayonnaise (below)
2 tablespoons chopped tarragon or parsley
4 spring onions (scallions), finely chopped

Remove the skin from the chicken and take all the flesh off the bones. Separate the chicken meat into bite-sized slivers. Put them into a bowl with the celery, apple, walnuts, salt and pepper and mix gently.

Mix together the soured cream, mayonnaise, chopped herb and spring onions and fold the mixture into the chicken salad.
Serves 6

Mayonnaise

Homemade mayonnaise will keep in a screw-top jar in the refrigerator for two weeks. Your kitchen equipment must be spotless, the eggs fresh and at room temperature and you must be careful to add the oil drop by drop at the beginning of the liaison. It is quite magical to make the first time.

2 egg yolks
1 teaspoon French mustard
¼ teaspoon salt

250 ml/8 fl oz/1 cup olive oil
1 tablespoon lemon juice

Beat together the egg yolks, mustard and salt. Add the oil, drop by drop, beating all the time. You can use a whisk, an electric beater or a food processor. As the mayonnaise thickens, you can add the oil in larger quantities. If the mayonnaise curdles, put a fresh egg yolk in a clean bowl and start again, dripping the curdled mayonnaise in drop by drop. When thick, add the lemon juice and stir in with a wooden spoon. You may need to add more lemon juice or hot water after it has been stored for a while, as it will thicken up again.
Makes about 250 ml/8 fl oz/1 cup

Chicken Sandwiches. Waldorf Chicken Salad makes a great filling for hearty sandwiches. Chop the ingredients finer than you would for the salad and omit the soured cream to make a drier filling. Butter the bread if liked and spread one side with the waldorf chicken filling. Press the slices together and cut into 2 or 4 wedges. This filling also tastes good in crusty bread sticks.

Waldorf Chicken Salad served in a cos (romaine) lettuce leaf. If you have never tasted it, you and your family are in for a real culinary treat.

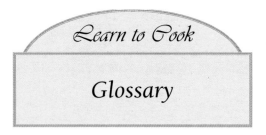

Learn to Cook

Glossary

Baste: Spoon pan juice over food while it is cooking to keep it from going dry and to crisp the skin.

Bind: Add an egg or liquid to a food mixture to hold it together.

Blanch: Immerse food briefly in boiling water to soften it or to remove skin.

Bouquet garni: A combination of fresh bay leaf, thyme and parsley tied with string or, if dried, tied up in a muslin (cheesecloth) bag. Used to flavour soups, casseroles and braised dishes, stocks, poached and boiled dishes and sauces.

Clarified butter: Pure butterfat which will reach a high temperature for frying without burning (p. 22).

Deglaze: Scrape the tasty sediment off the bottom of a pan with the help of wine, stock or cream, to make sauces and gravies.

Degrease: Skim the fat off the surface of a sauce, stock or casserole (p. 14).

Doneness: State of being adequately cooked. You can tell whether a piece of poultry is done by inserting a skewer into the thickest part of the flesh—if the juice runs clear without any pinkness, it is cooked.

Dredge: Coat meat lightly with flour and seasonings (p. 35).

Dress: Make poultry ready for cooking by cleaning and trussing (pp. 14, 42).

Escalopes: Thin, even slices of chicken or turkey breast which can be pan-fried just like veal escalopes.

Jointed: Cut up into serving pieces, either before or after cooking (pp. 20, 28).

Marinate: Soak raw ingredients in a liquid to preserve them and to make them more tender, using wine, oil, vinegar, lemon juice, herbs and spices.

Olive oil: Oil extracted from the fruit of the olive tree. The first cold pressing of the olives is the extra virgin oil and the highest quality flavour. Every pressing after that gives lower and lower standards of oil. The earlier the pressing, the better the flavour. Olive oil can be used as a cooking fat with butter or instead of butter.

Preheated oven: An oven that has been turned on in sufficient time for it to have reached the desired temperature when you require it. Most ovens will take about 15 minutes to heat.

Reduce: Thicken a liquid by rapid boiling, which reduces the quantity of the liquid and concentrates the flavours. Sauces are often thickened by reduction.

Shallot: A member of the onion family, smaller than the common onion and more delicate in flavour. Like garlic, the bulbs separate into cloves. If shallots are unavailable, you can substitute green onions (scallions or spring onions).

Simmer: Keeping a liquid just below boiling point so that it 'shivers'.

Skim: Remove the scum from a liquid after it comes to the boil, usually with a large spoon or a flat sieve.

Stock: Liquid made by simmering meat and vegetables in water for over 3 hours to extract the flavour (p. 44). Used to enhance the flavour of sauces and soups.

Sweat: Soften vegetables by cooking them gently in butter or oil until they release their juices but do not brown.

Truss: Tie a bird with string into a neat shape for cooking (p. 42).

Vinegar: Produced by acetic fermentation in wine or cider, it can also be flavoured by herbs, spices, shallots and garlic or raspberries. Balsamic vinegar is an aged vinegar (10–50 years) with a wonderful delicate flavour.